ILLUSTRATED BIOGRAPHY FOR KIDS

THOMAS EDISON

EXTRAORDINARY SCIENTIST

WHO CHANGED THE WORLD

Wonder House

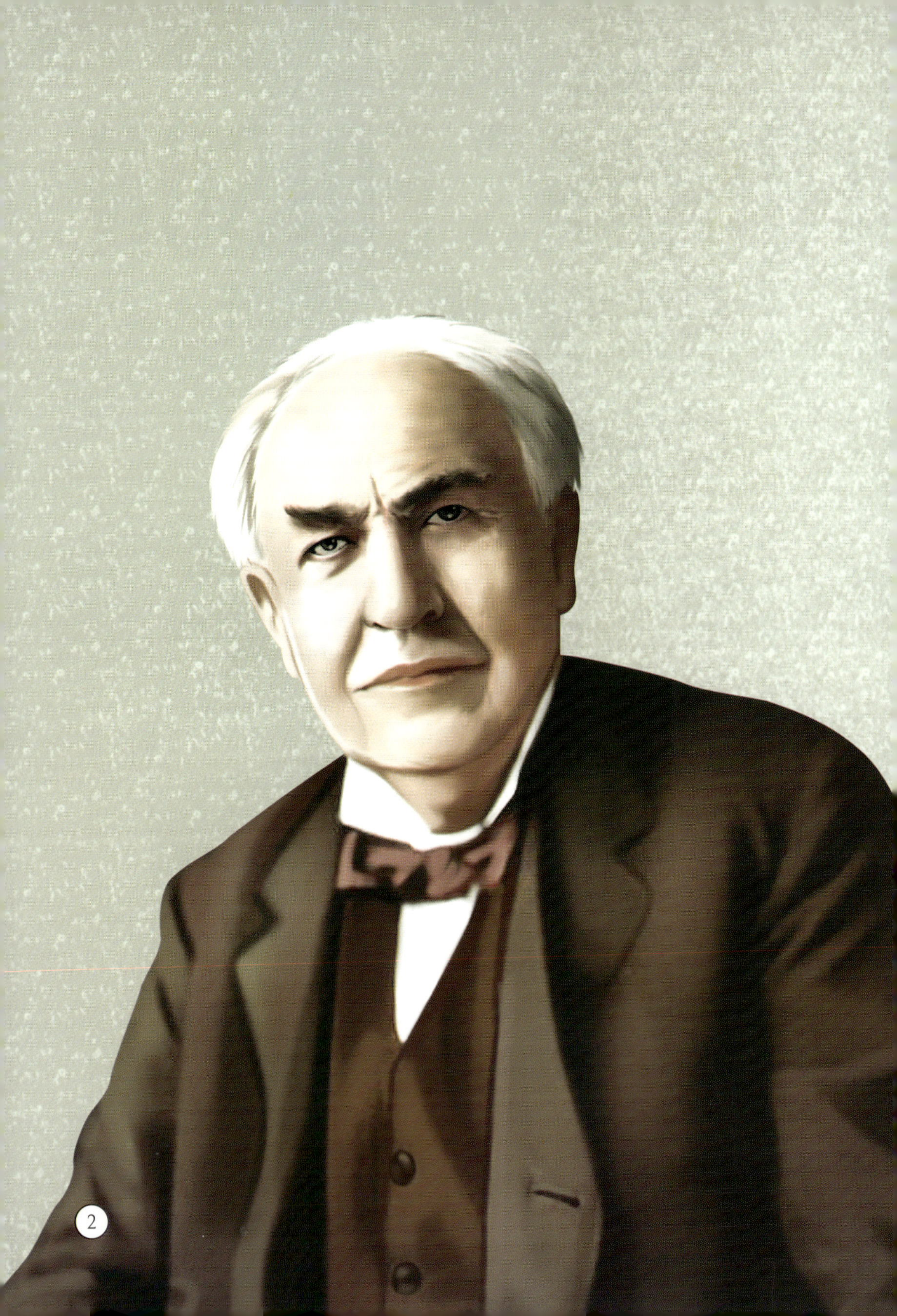

EDISON: THE CLASSIC GENIUS

Thomas Alva Edison was an American investor, manufacturer and businessman, best known for his inventions of the incandescent light bulb, the phonograph, the motion picture camera and electric power generation. He is also credited with the improvements of the means of communication; the improved versions of the telephone and telegraph.

Edison's remarkable inventions are a boon to the modern industrialized world, his undeniable presence and ingenuity formed the bedrock for modern scientific discoveries. His widespread impact can be gauged through the organization and structure he brought to the field of sciences. With more than 1,093 patents to his name, he brought the idea of organized research and the power of teamwork to the forefront. He built the first industrial research laboratory at Menlo Park and brought researchers, assistants, engineers, technicians and machinists under the same roof.

LITTLE SCIENTIST IN THE BASEMENT

Thomas Edison was born to Samuel Edison Jr and Nancy Elliott on 11 February 1847 in Milan, Ohio. He was the youngest of the seven children born to his parents, of which only four survived to adulthood. He spent most of his childhood in Port Huron, Michigan, where his family moved in 1854. He spent only a few months in school and learned basic reading, writing and arithmetic from his mother, who was a school teacher. From early childhood, he was fascinated with scientific experiments and discoveries.

At a very young age, he built a small chemistry laboratory in the basement of his house. But these early adventures didn't go well with his mother, who was anxious that his little scientist may set the house on fire! At the age of 12, Edison suffered from hearing loss. But this inability didn't deter him from achieving new heights, more often he talked of this disability as a blessing in disguise; it enabled him to concentrate more on his work, devoid of any external distractions.

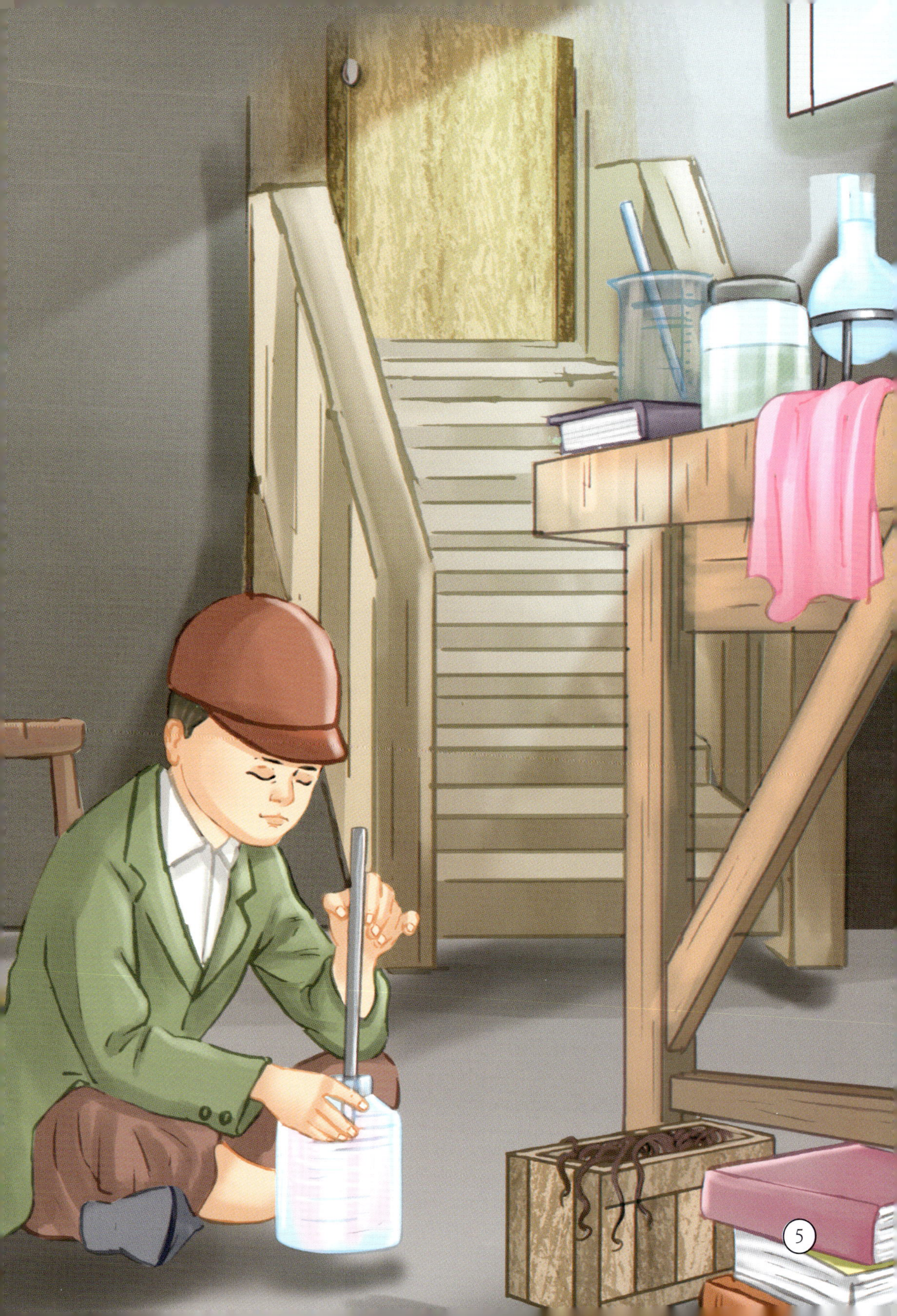

YOUNG ENTREPRENEUR

At the age of 13, Edison started making his own way into the world. He began by selling snacks, candies and newspapers to the passengers traveling on the local railroad line from Port Huron to Detroit. During the Battle of Shiloh, he estimated that he would be able to sell the extra copies, so he bought thousands of copies

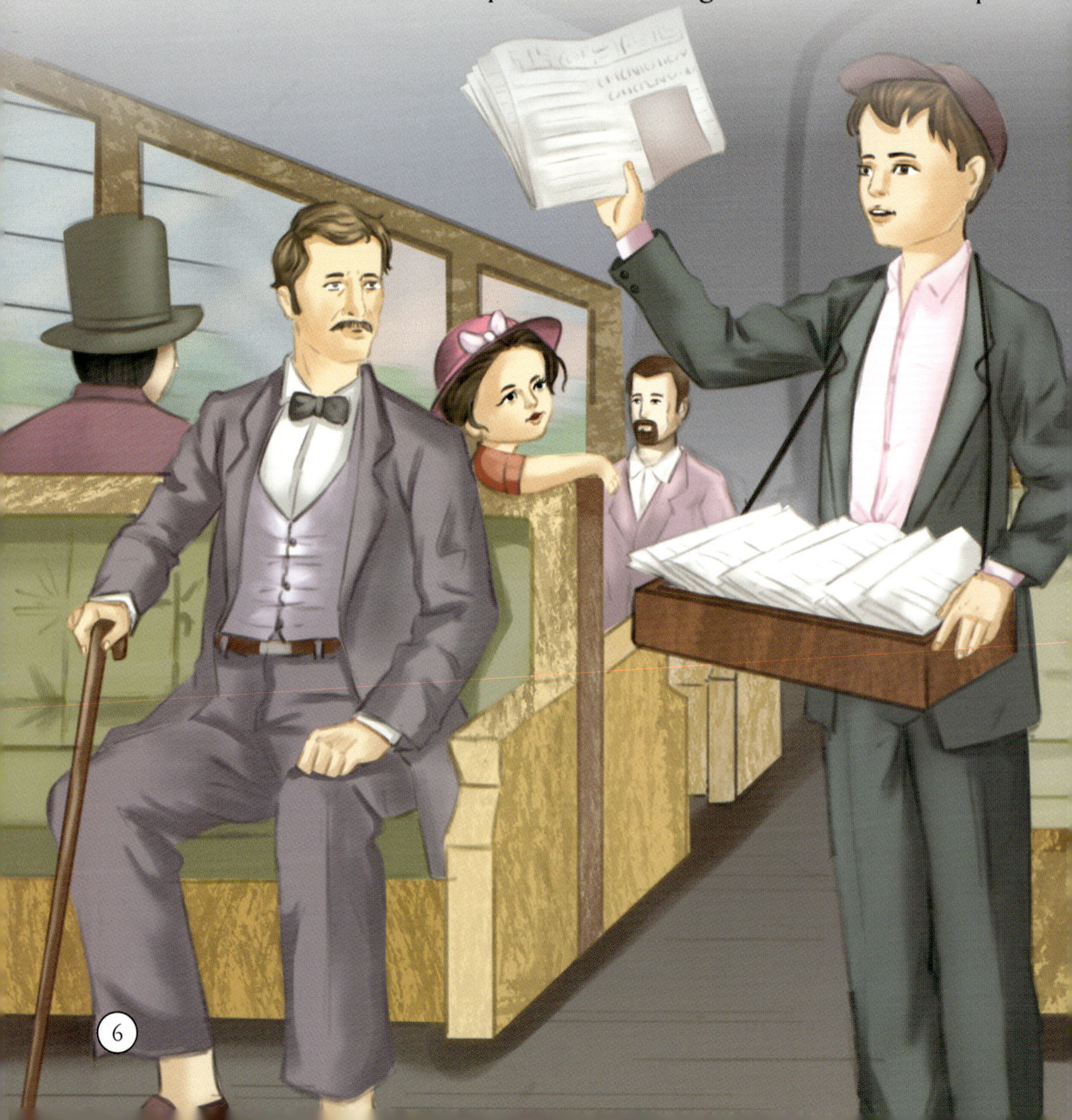

of newspapers in advance for sale. He was banking on his instincts and reason, and raised the prices as he moved away from the railway line, giving the first glimpse of his great entrepreneurial skills.

Soon, he brought a portable printing press on a moving train and started printing his own newspaper. This venture was so successful that its circulation rose week by week. The money earned from these ventures was used into buying scientific equipments for his new laboratory, which was set up in the baggage car of a train.

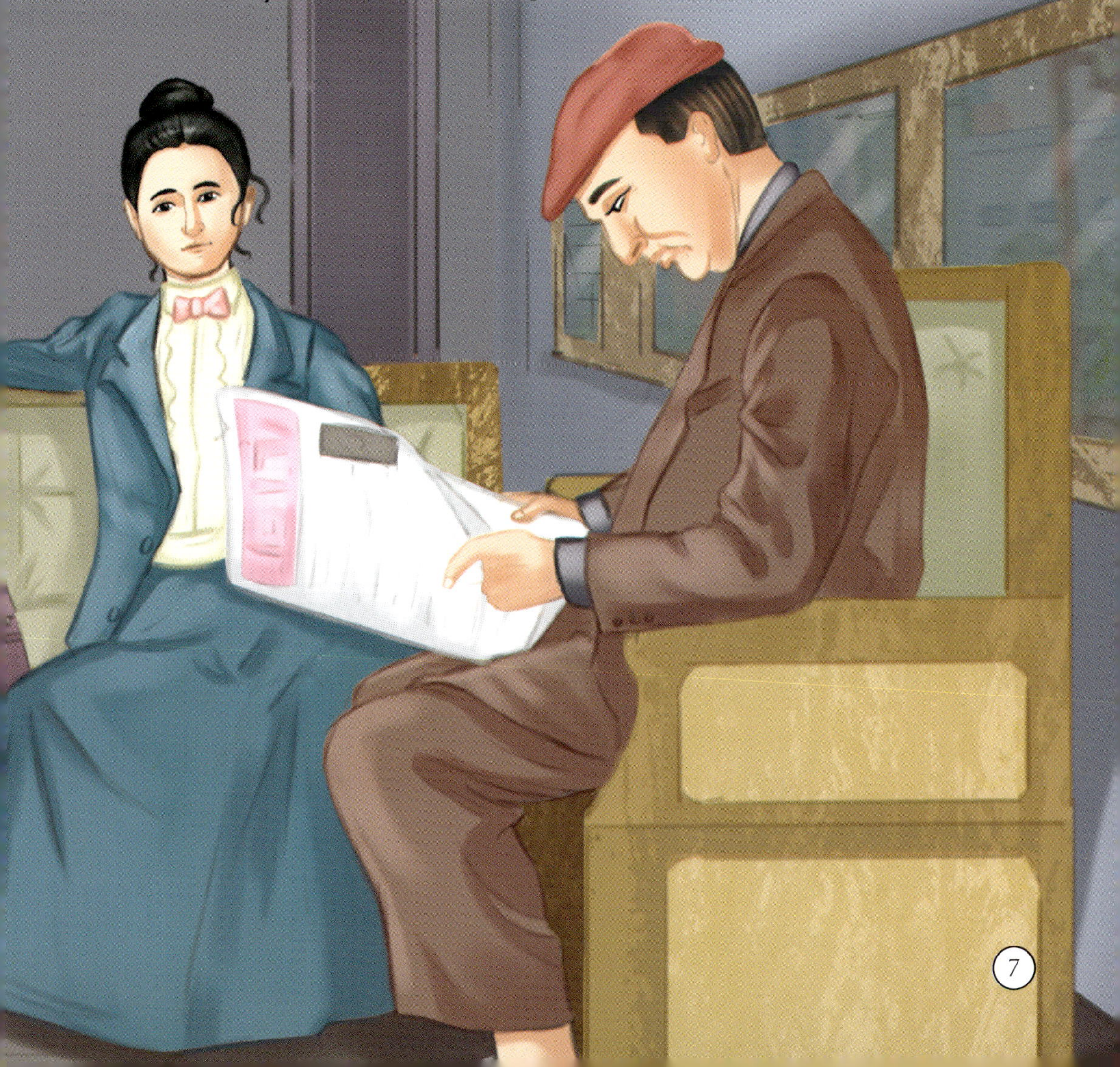

AS TELEGRAPHER

Edison became a telegraph operator after he saved a station master's son's life: one day Edison saw a young boy—son of a station master—playing on the train tracks. The boy was

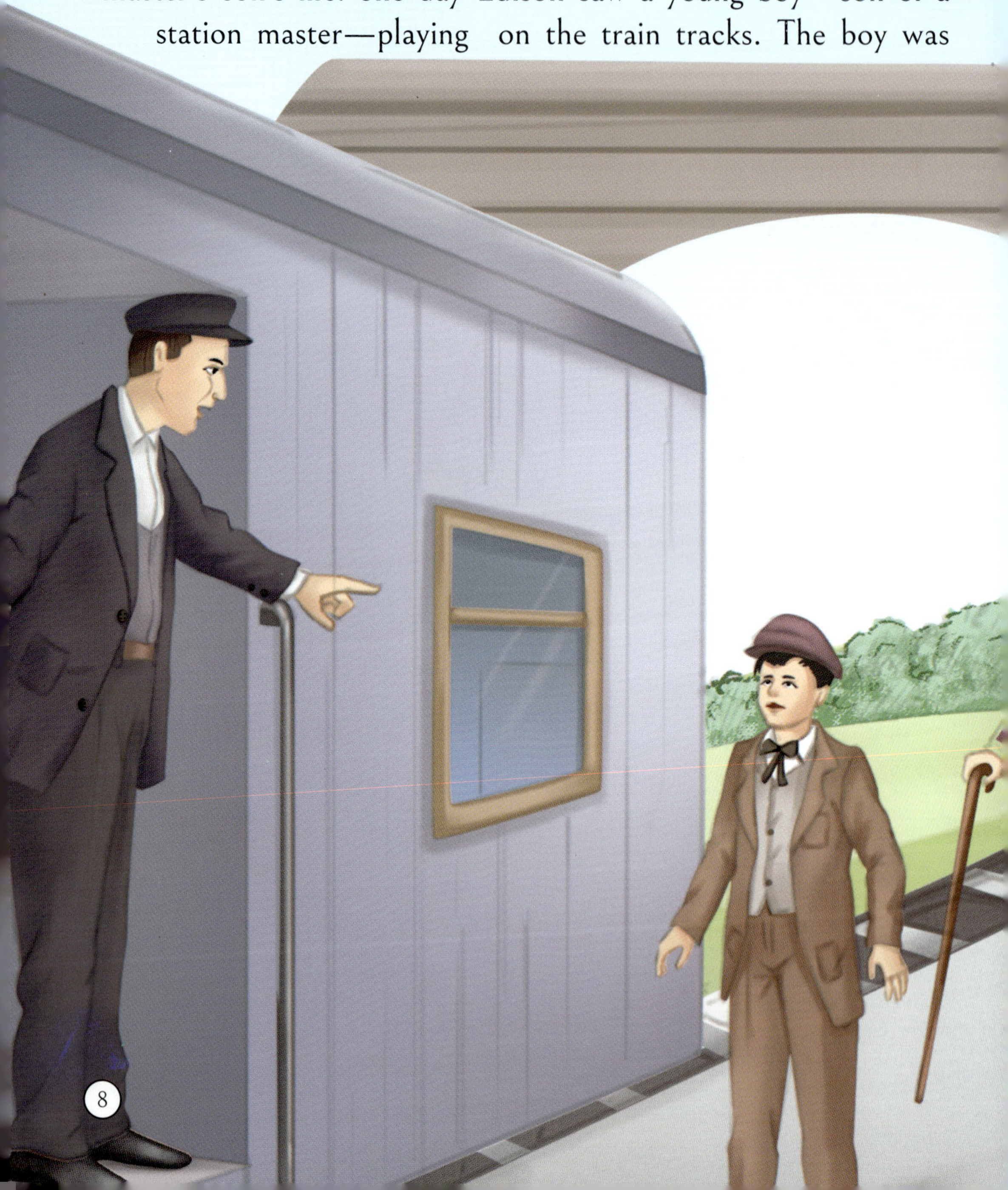

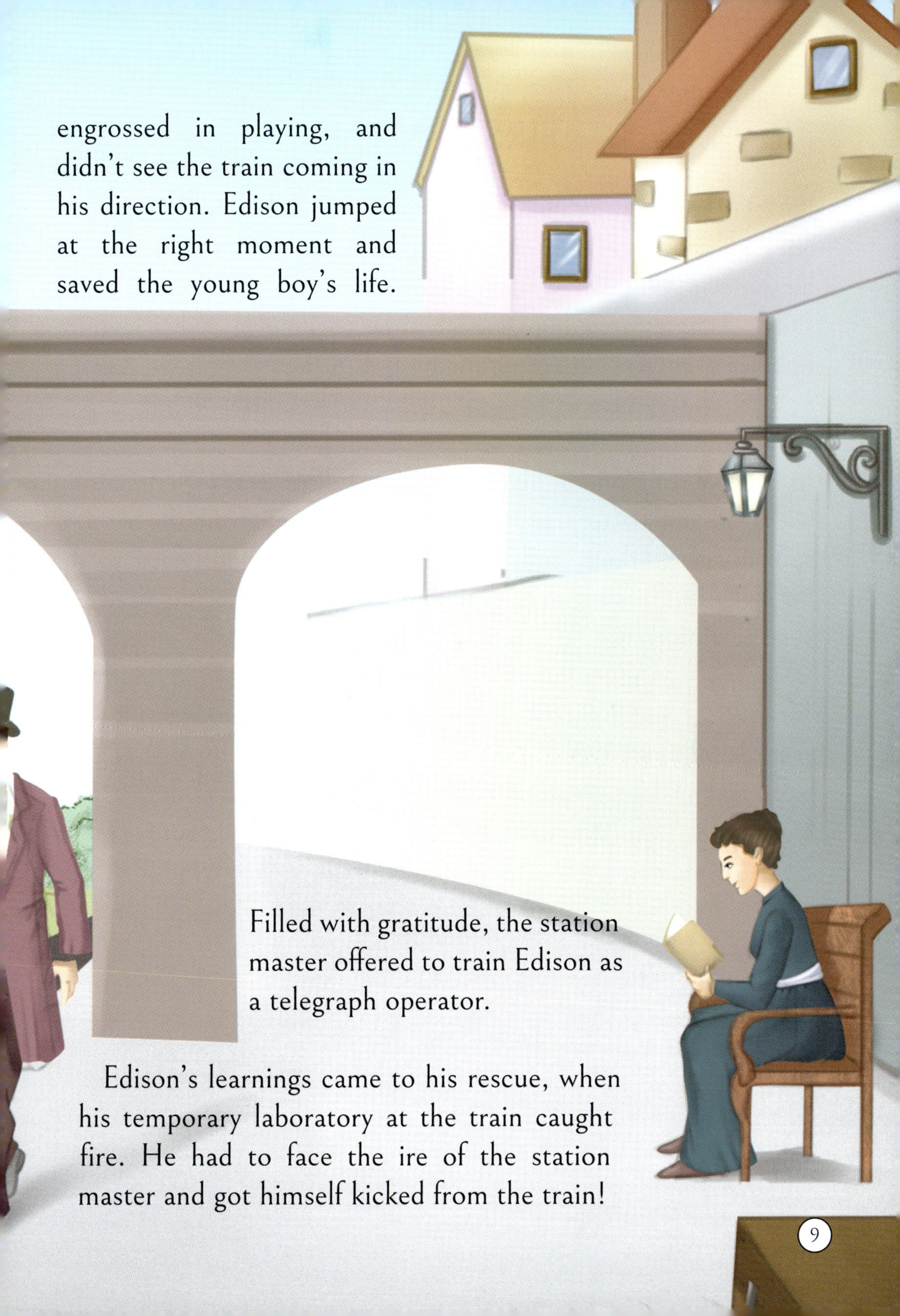

engrossed in playing, and didn't see the train coming in his direction. Edison jumped at the right moment and saved the young boy's life.

Filled with gratitude, the station master offered to train Edison as a telegraph operator.

Edison's learnings came to his rescue, when his temporary laboratory at the train caught fire. He had to face the ire of the station master and got himself kicked from the train!

FIRST PATENT

For the next few years, Edison took job at Western Union as telegraph operator and widely traveled across the country. During his time in Western Union, Edison requested to work in night shifts. This allowed him enough time to indulge in his favorite hobbies of reading and experimenting. But these indulgences came at a very heavy price.

In 1867, during one of his night shifts, Edison was experimenting with lead-acid battery, some of the sulphuric acid from the battery, spilled on the floor, and percolated from the floorboard to his boss's desk. This incident cost him his job, and he was fired the very next morning.

In 1869, Edison patented his first invention: an electric vote recorder, this new invention eliminated the need for manual roll calls and instantly tallied the votes. But it didn't impress the legislatures, who felt it robbed them of lobbying for votes among all the confusion and noises!

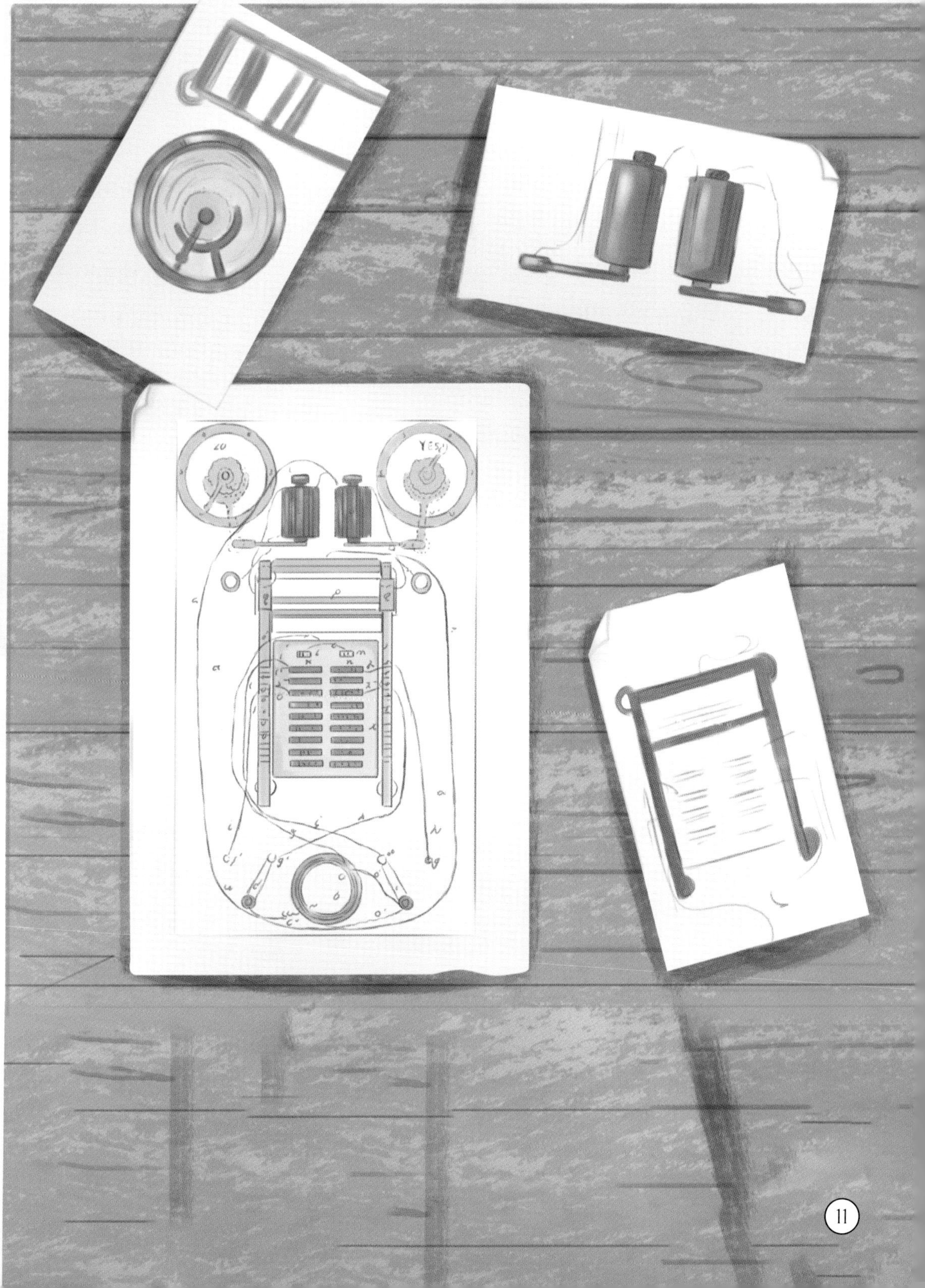

MENLO PARK

Edison's most significant invention was the establishment of a research development facility, known as Menlo Park. Alhough workshops for scientific research had existed in the past too, but Edison's effort to bring scientists, researchers, employees and engineers together under the same roof, was an idea that was completely new and revolutionary at the same time. For little did Edison know that his model would later be adopted by various institutions in the future!

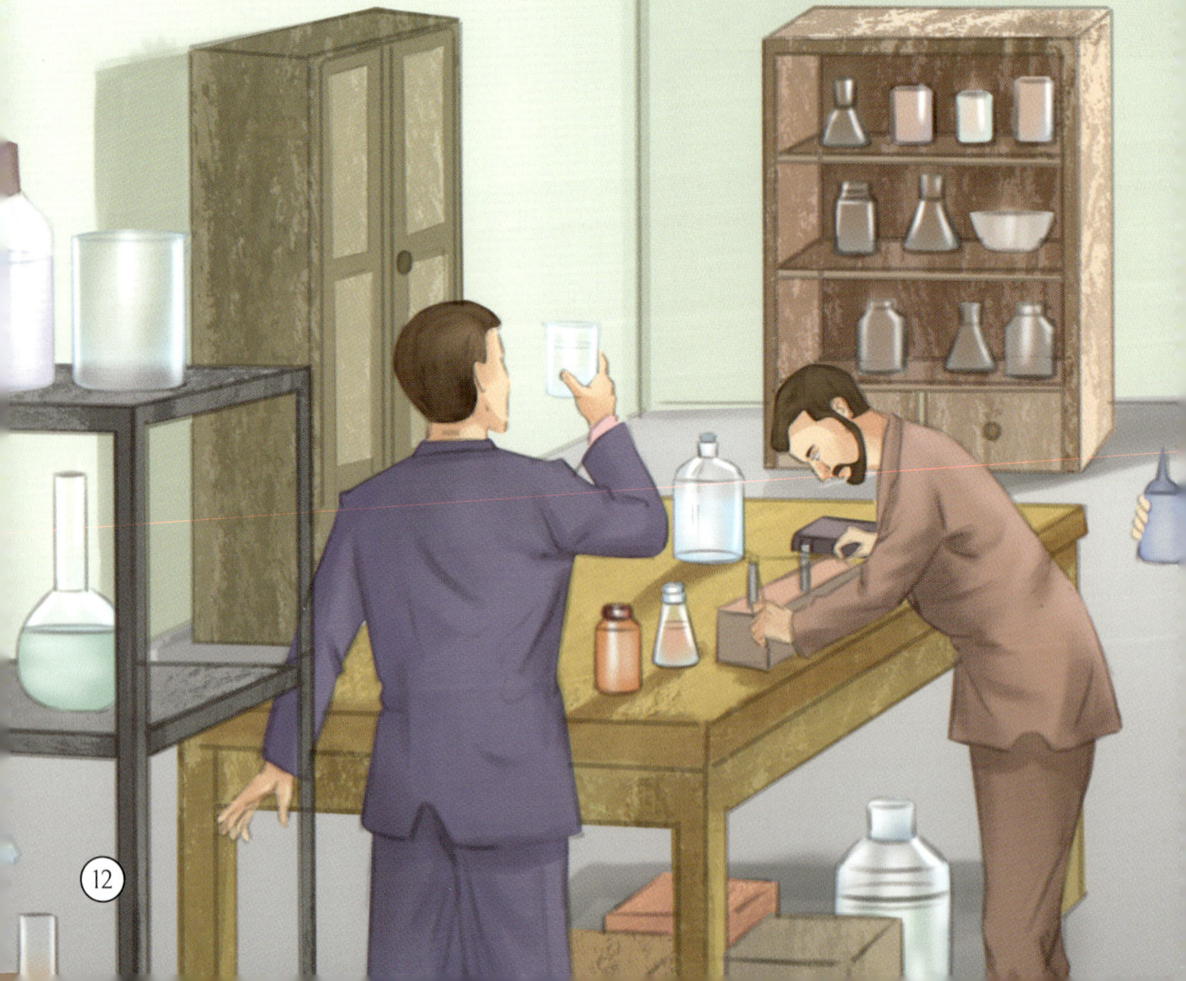

Edison's idea behind the research development facility was to divide the problems into small parts and use expertise from different fields of study to solve that problem and bring together a feasible solution. Then, these parts were brought together as a whole and a new discovery came into being.

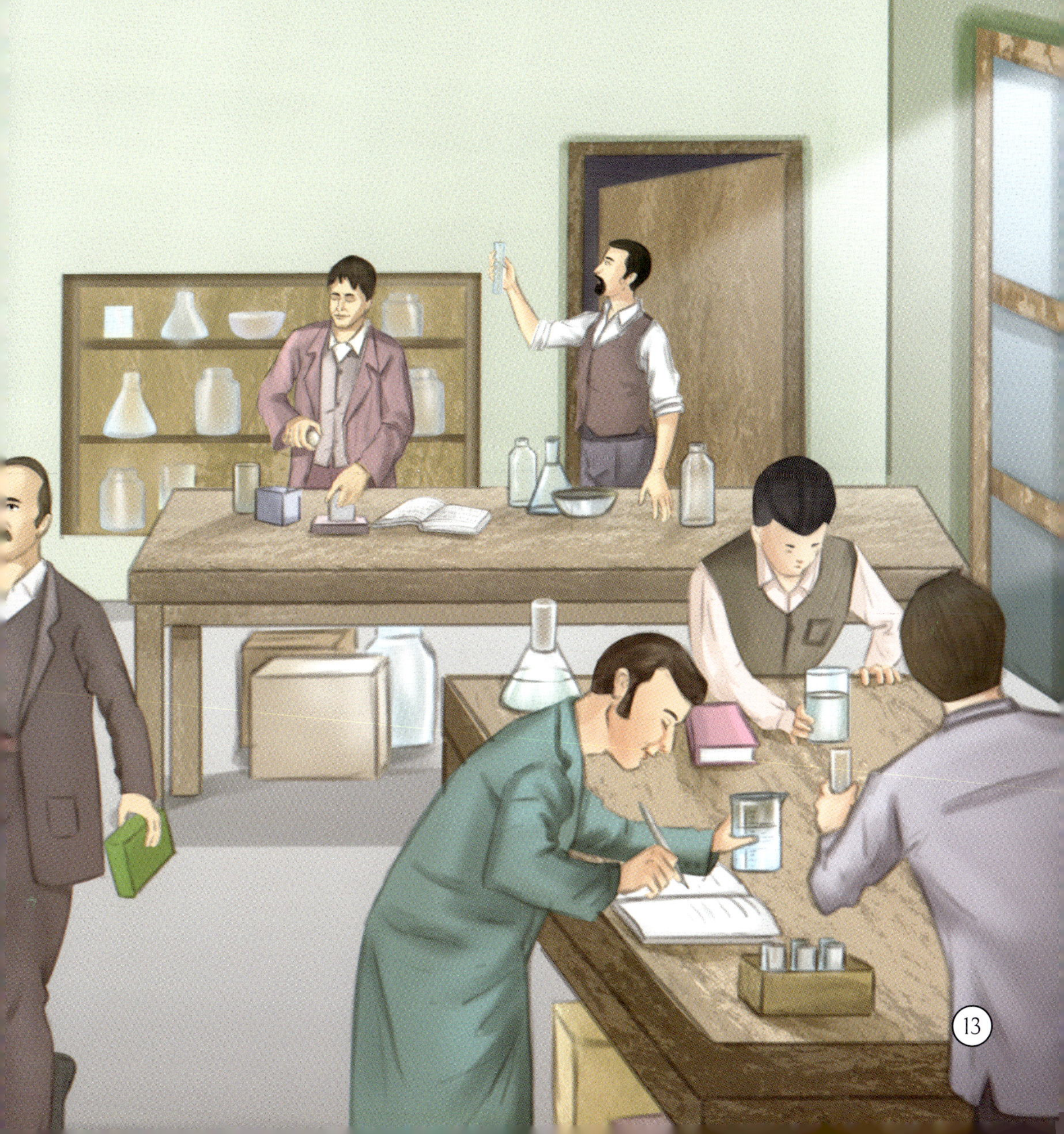

INVENTION OF PHONOGRAPH

The failure of Edison's electric vote recorder shaped his vision to look for more practical and profitable inventions. He understood that people wanted fast and quick solutions to their problems. Thus, taking a cue from the demand, he changed his perspective of research on the practical demand of the masses.

He decided to invest more in improving the already invented devices and made huge profits from those improved models. He invested the money earned from these inventions, into his research development facility and his other businesses, showcasing his prowess as an entrepreneur.

In 1871, Edison married sixteen-year-old, Mary Stilwell, and with her, he raised three children. His discoveries gained a wider audience after his invention of the phonograph in 1877. This invention was so thrilling that Edison earned the name 'The Wizard of Menlo Park'. Interestingly, the first audio recording on phonograph was Edison singing 'Mary Had a Little Lamb' for his kids!

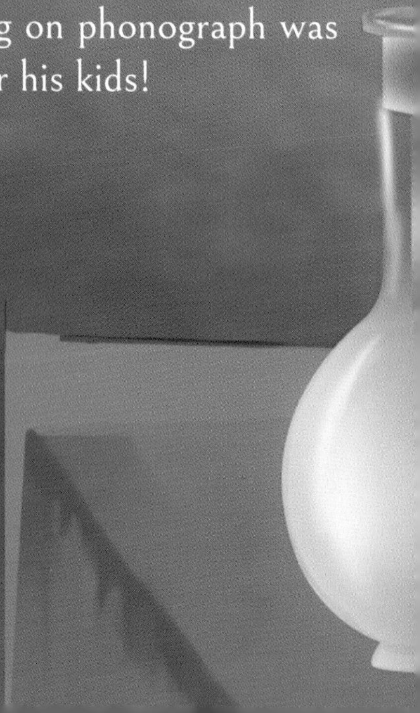

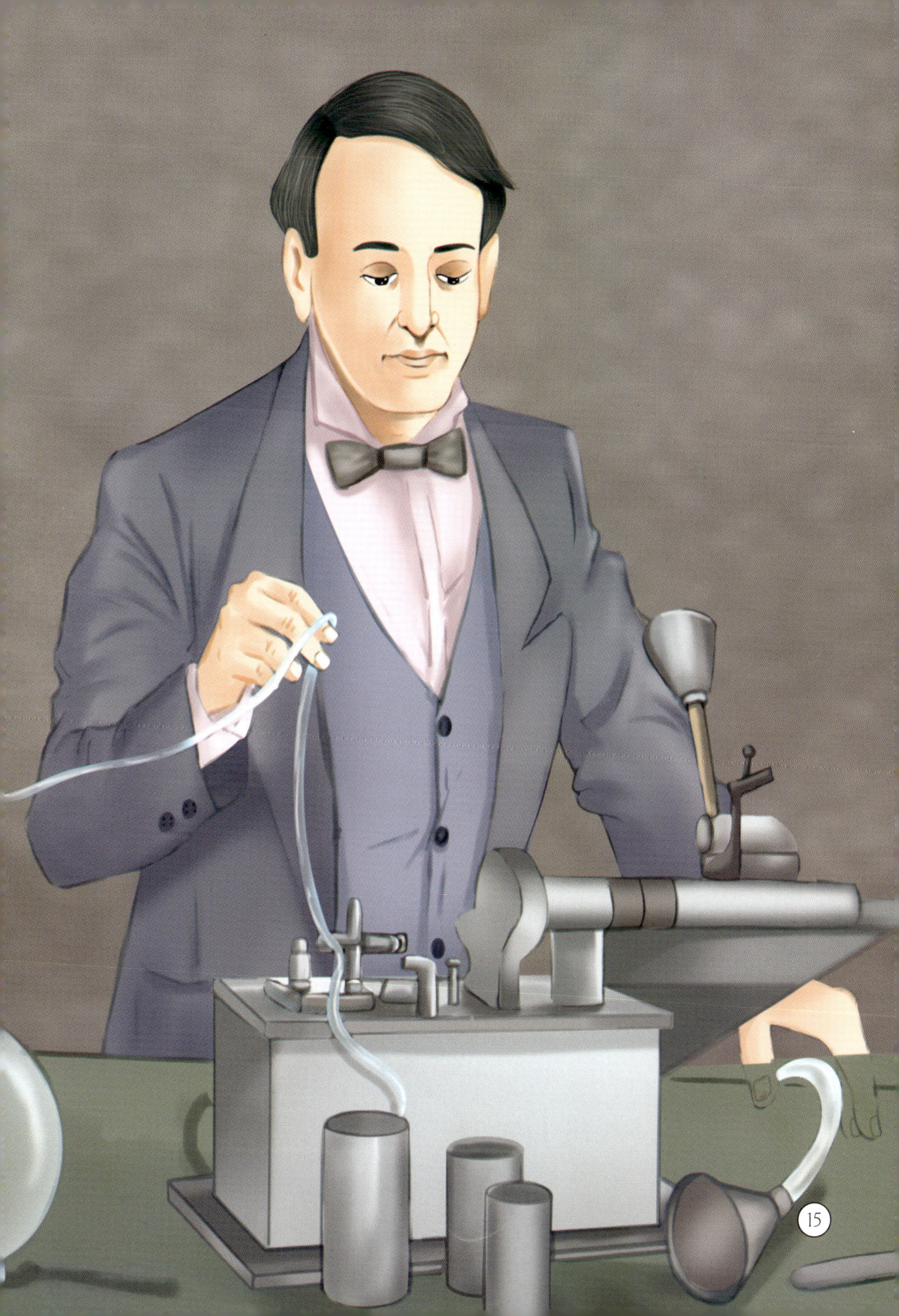

Edison came up with the idea of a phonograph while working on the improvements of Alexander Graham Bell's model of the telephone transmitter. He developed a carbon microphone, for the purpose of better sound quality at long distances. At first, what he aimed, was to make a machine that could transcribe the calls, but later realized that recording sound in itself was possible too.

His invention of the phonograph was such a success that many investors poured in their money to finance Edison's discoveries. With the new money coming in, Edison opened gates of his research development facility to new talents, and many more engineers and technicians were hired. This team of skillful men, often called 'muckers', created a plethora of scientific wonders, most of which are in use till today.

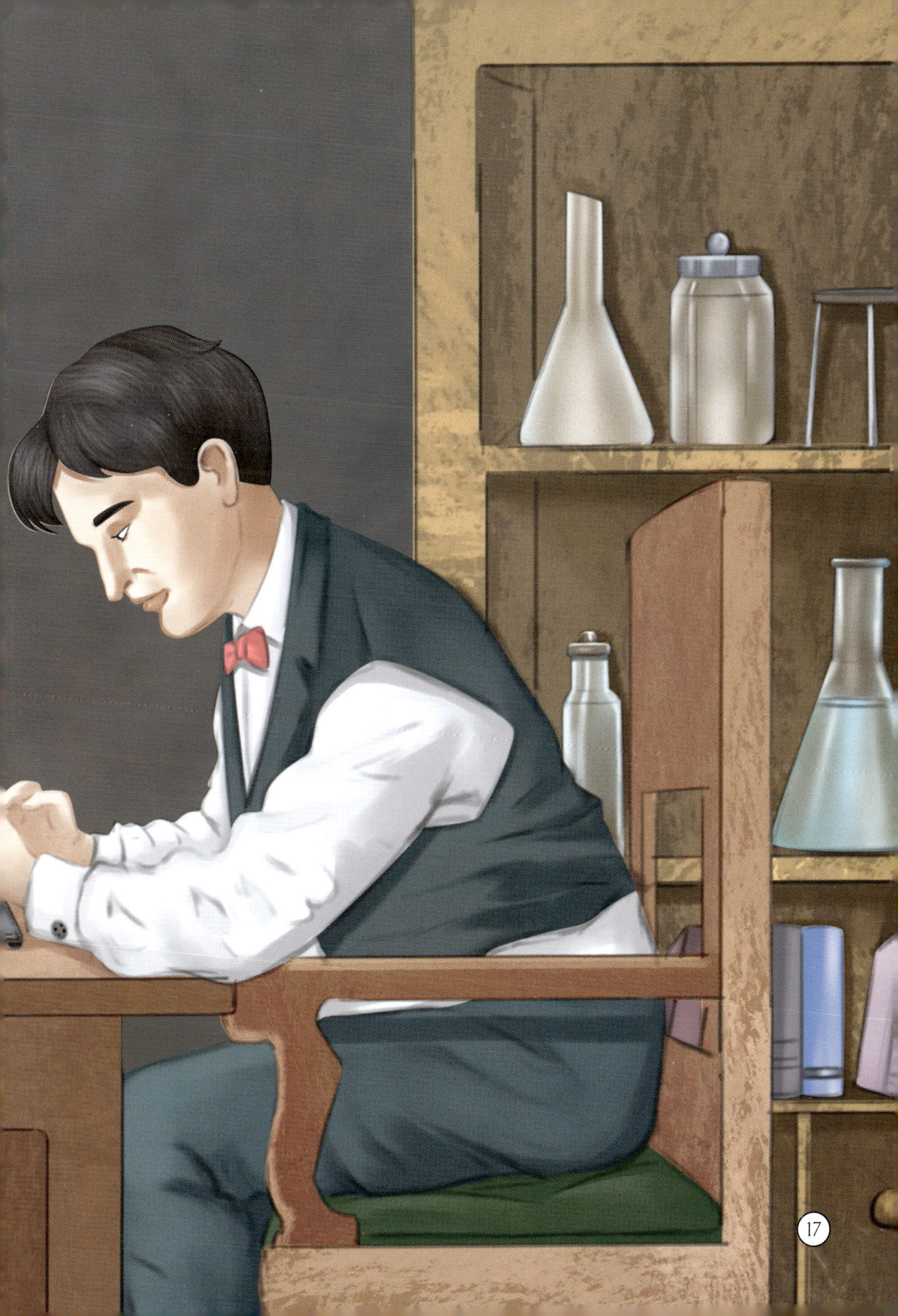

IMPROVED INCANDESCENT LAMP

Edison earned worldwide fame for his improvement of the incandescent light bulb. Earlier in the 1870s, homes were lit by indoor gas lamps. These indoor lamps were often called 'Lamps of Nightmares'; they were not only irritating to the eye but produced sooty fumes too.

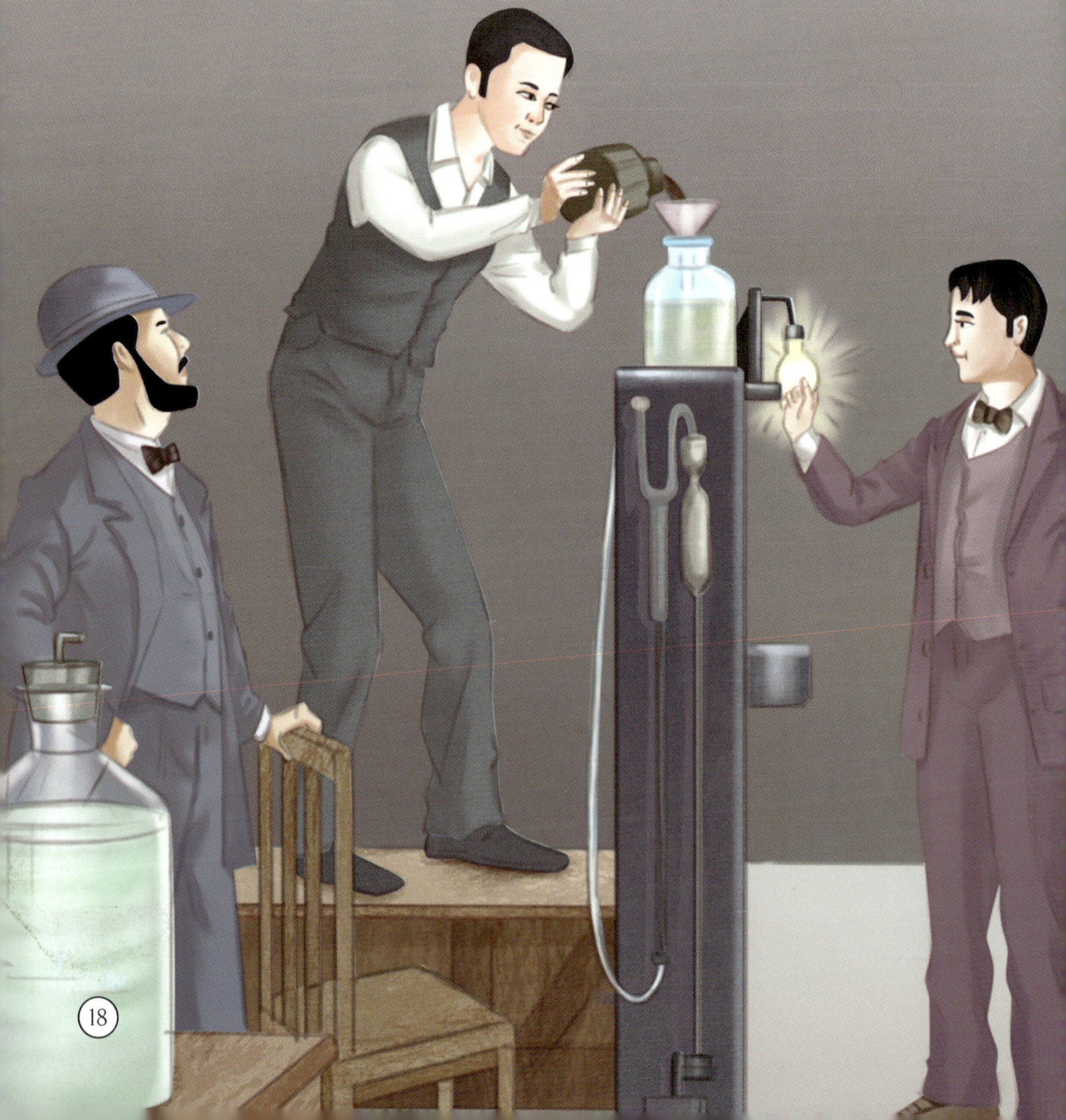

The earlier models of bulbs used platinum filaments, and the high cost of platinum, came in their way of being a household success. These early models also suffered from the problems of extremely short life and the usage of high electricity for their operation.

Edison and his team understood these issues on ground and with his team of engineers, he looked for solutions to make improvements in the early models of incandescent lamps, that would allow light bulbs to burn longer at a reliable brightness.

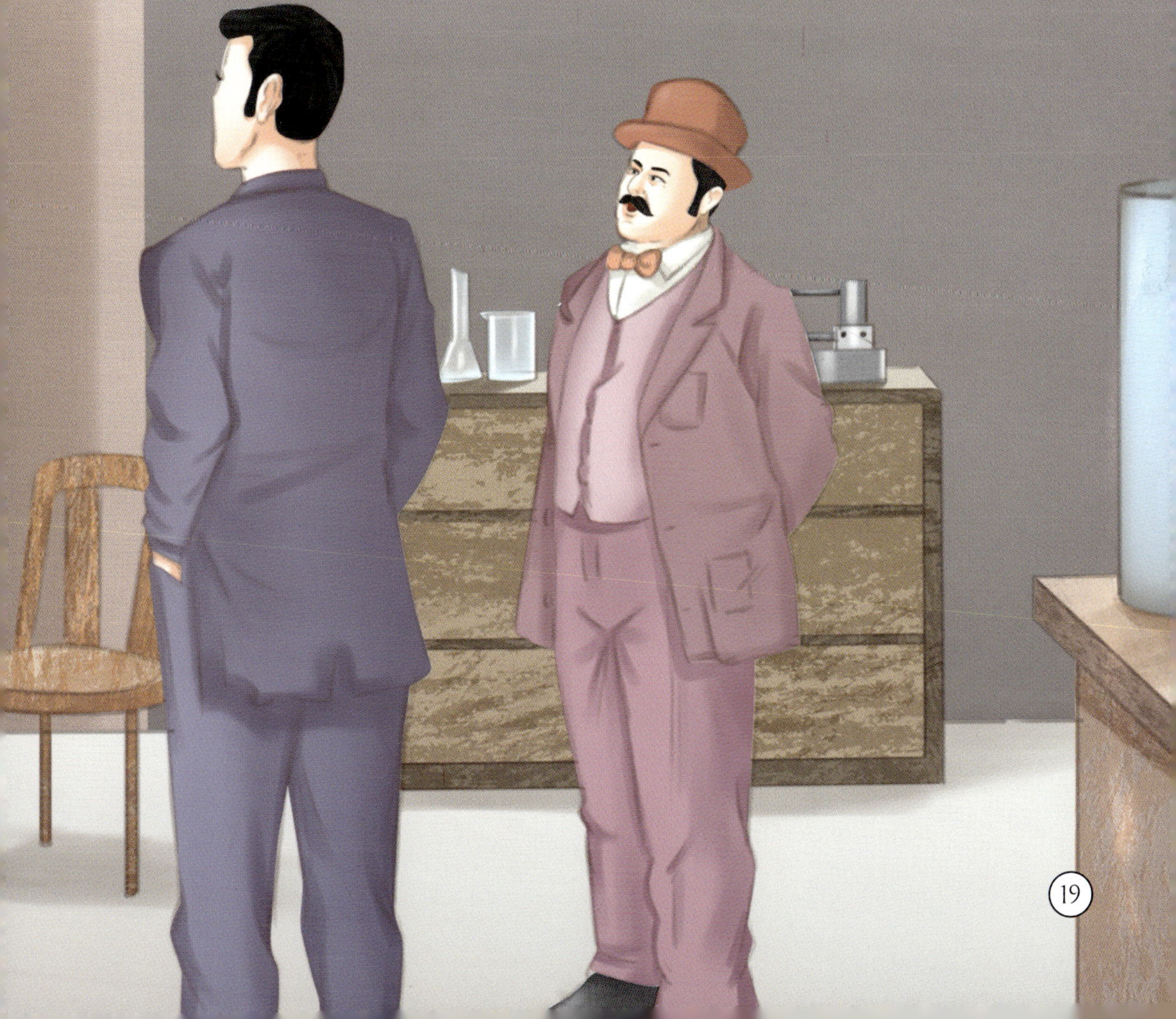

The most challenging affair in improving these light bulbs was choosing the right material for the filament. Edison tried experimenting with various materials and at last settled on carbon. This carbon filament burned for about fifteen hours. A year later, Edison and his team experimented with carbonized bamboo, which burned for more than a thousand hours.

So remarkable was this discovery at the time, that hundreds of passengers would get down from the train just to witness the illuminated Menlo Park, brightened with a network of light bulbs. People were awed by the brightness of these light bulbs, it was a major change for them, as for the majority of them, the brightness was limited to the candle-lights. These new and improved light bulbs were not only soot-free but even stayed lit through winds and rains, and could be turned on and off with ease.

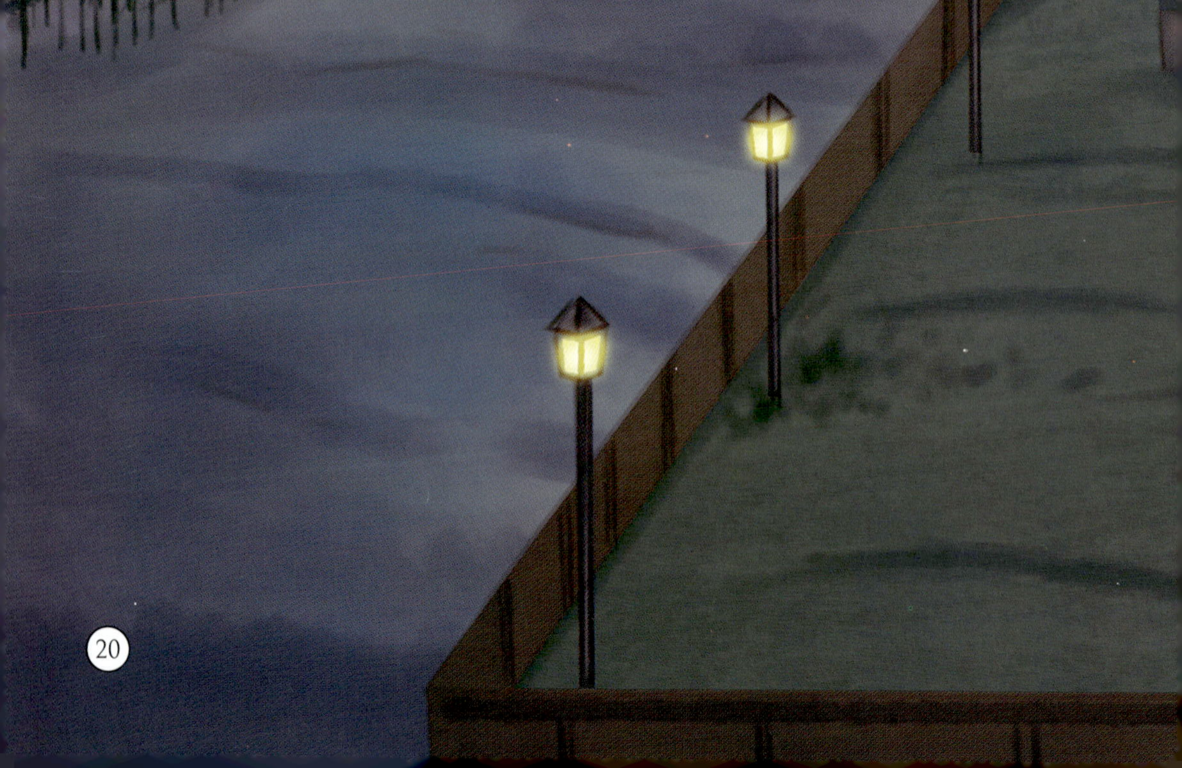

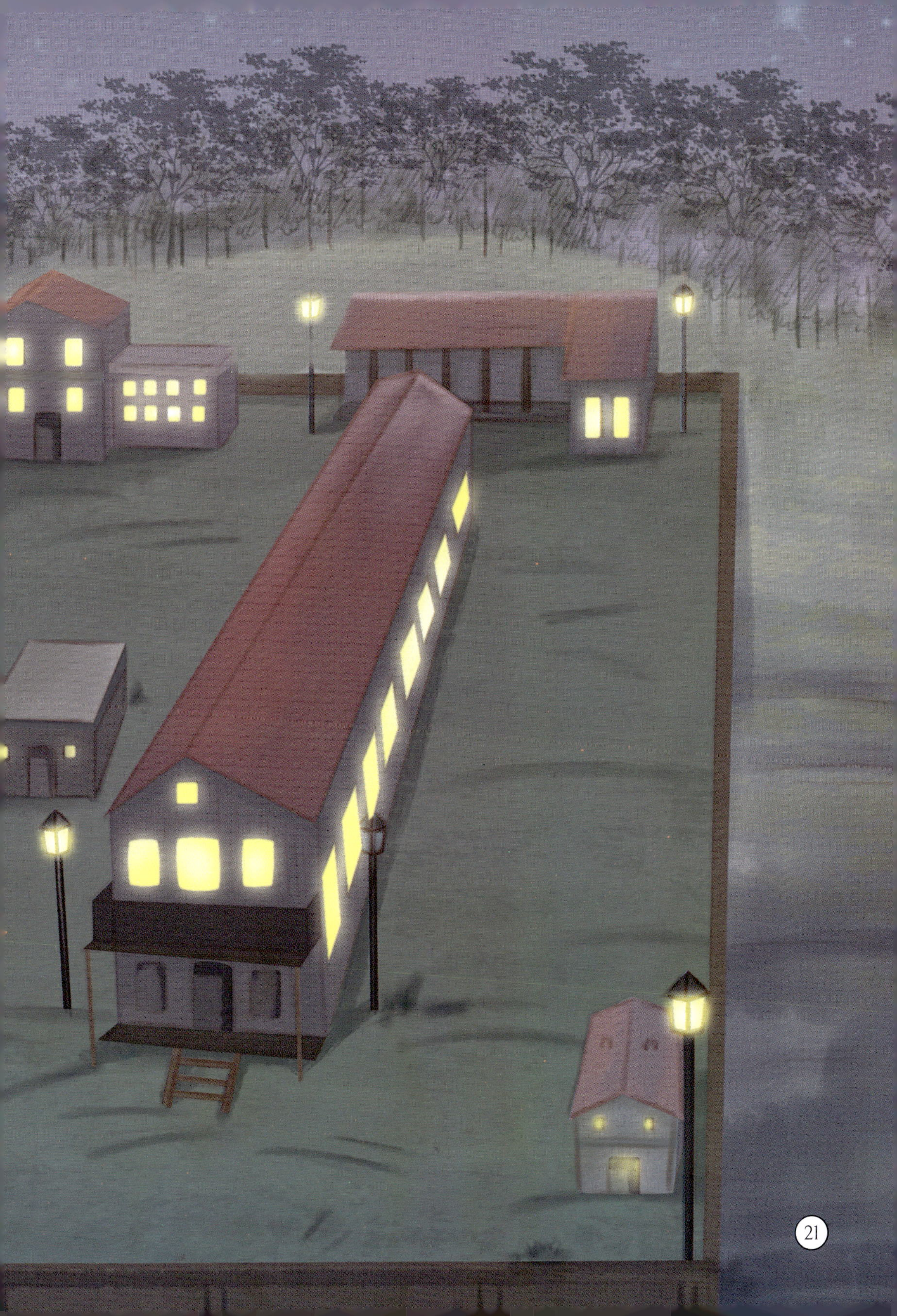

ELECTRIC POWER DISTRIBUTION

In 1880, Edison founded the Edison Illuminating Company and patented a system of electrical distribution. He used this electrical system to win the contract to electrify some parts of New York City. Later he went on to build an electricity generation plant on Pearl Street, which served the electricity needs of more than nine hundred customers.

However, these moments of success came with a period of grief. Edison's wife Mary died in the August of 1884. This was a major setback for Edison and his family. After his wife's death, Edison left Menlo Park. Two years later he married Mina Miller, and

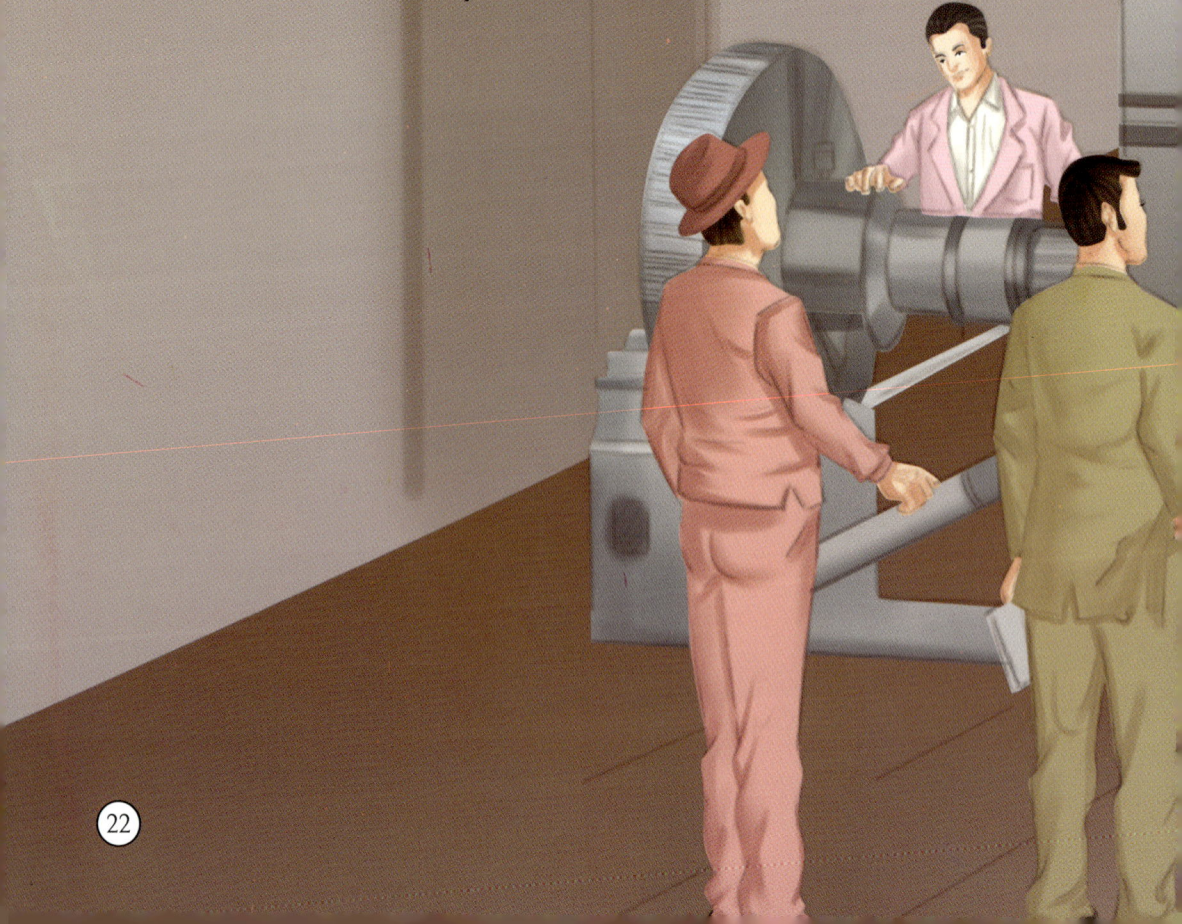

with her, he had three children. This time, he moved his family to West Orange, New Jersey, where he built another laboratory. This new laboratory was a major improvement from the one at Menlo Park.

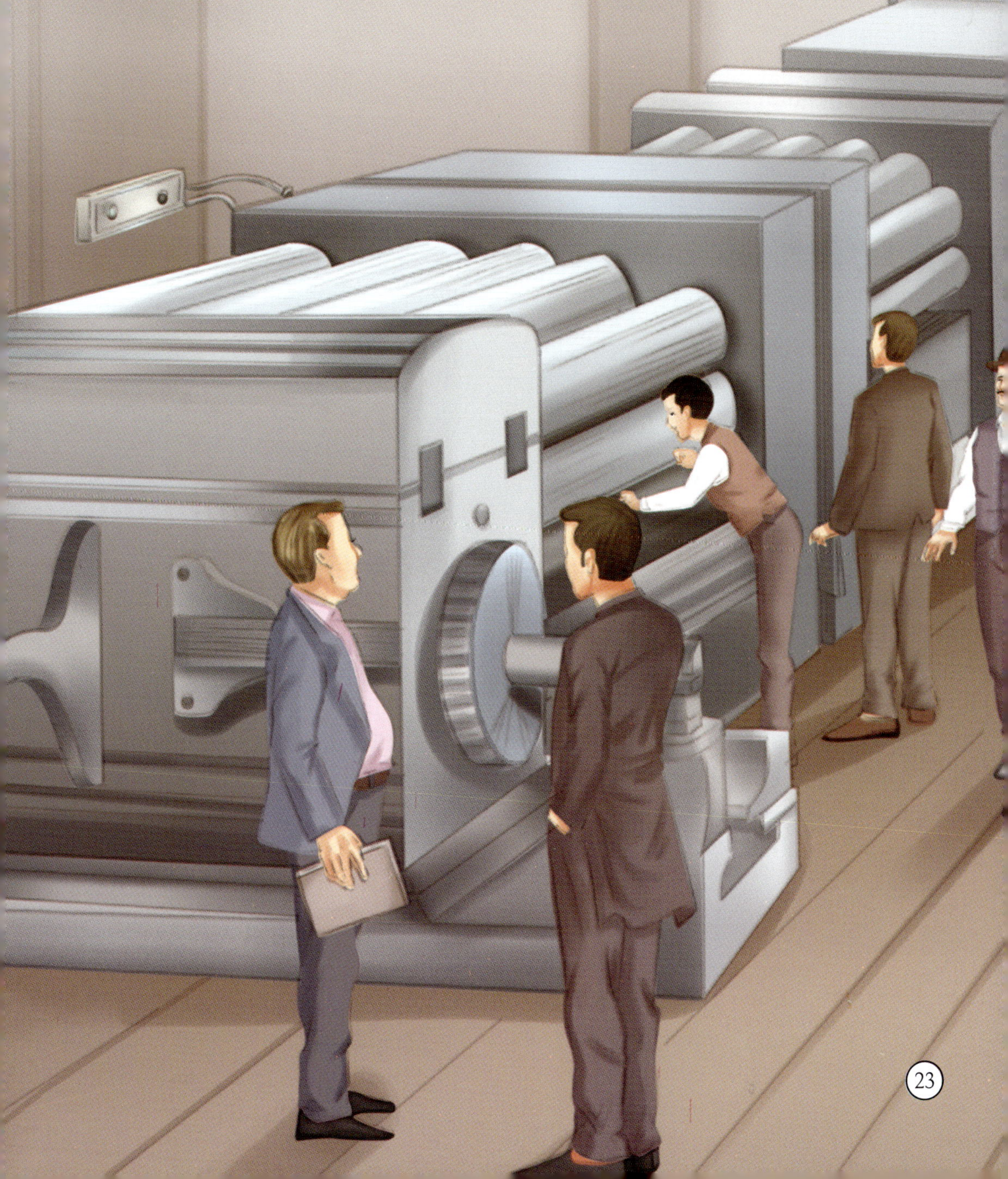

WAR OF CURRENTS

With the establishment of electrical distribution system, Edison received stiff competition from other companies in the market. In the 1880s, alternating current (AC) systems were gaining popularity among the masses. The major advantage of alternating currents was that they could be transmitted to longer distances with cheaper wires, and could extensively cover remote areas and villages.

On the other hand, Edison's DC voltage was only suitable for high-density areas, thus, leaving out a major chunk of the remote population in the darkness of night. Moreover, its high prices made it unaffordable for the smaller cities and rural areas.

This gap of inaccessibility and unaffordability paved the path for ACs to expand their business in the US. Soon, alternating current was used widely in street lighting and local businesses by the large population of domestic customers. The increased popularity of AC didn't go well with Edison. This became the reason of conflict between him and Nikola Tesla, the propagator of AC current.

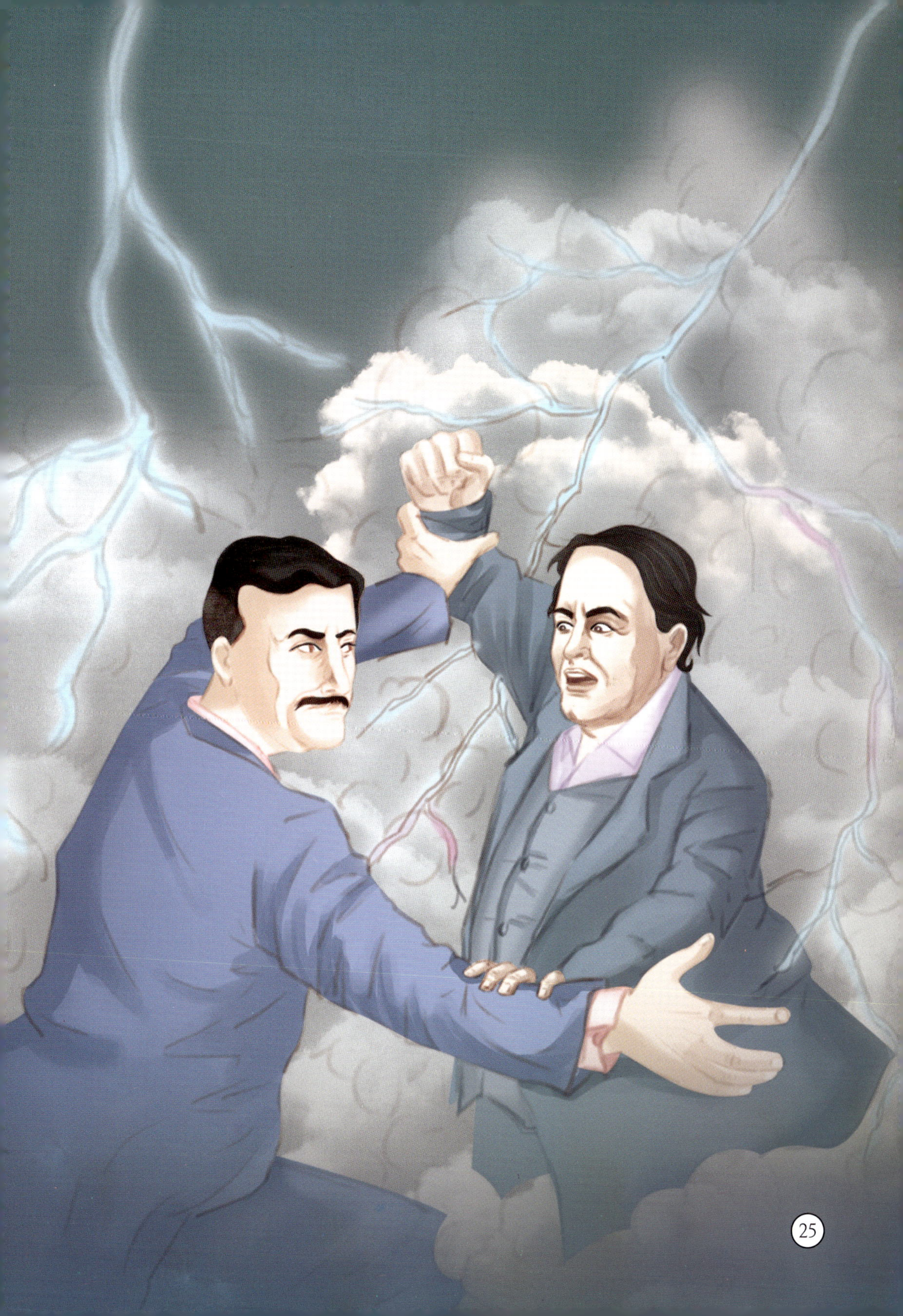

MOTION PICTURES AND OTHER INVENTIONS

Besides the incandescent lamp, Edison worked on myriad inventions and improved upon already-made models. He patented the early model of the motion picture camera, called the Kinetograph or Peep-hole viewer. The device became wildly famous among the masses, enabling them to watch short movies, while thoroughly entertaining them.

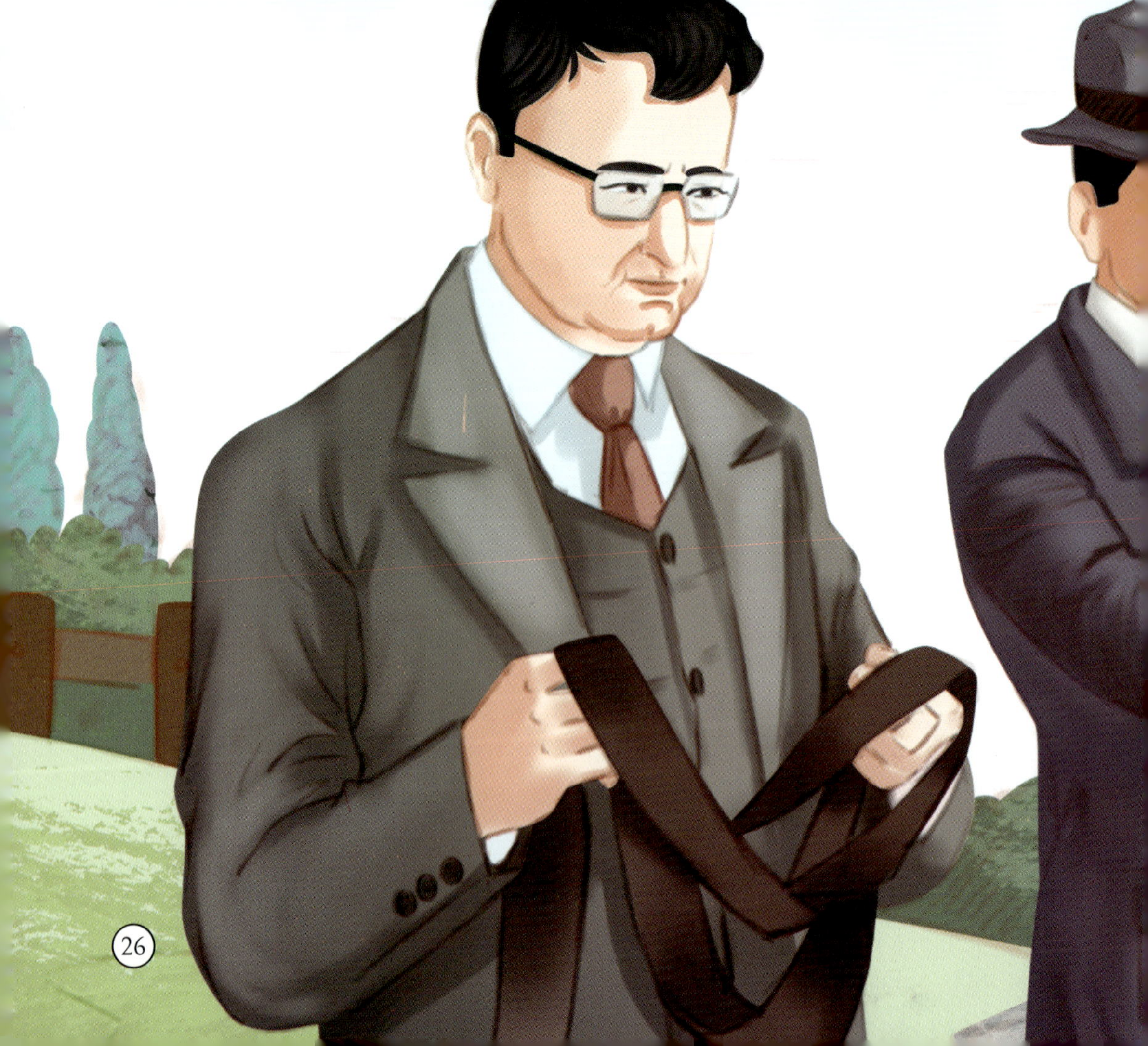

Edison is credited for the invention and development of many instruments such as the Tasimeter, for measuring infrared radiations and designed as well as produced the first commercially viable Fluoroscopy. His knowledge as a telegrapher helped him improve the early models of the Telegraph. He worked on developing lighter and more efficient models of rechargeable batteries and even ventured in the field of mining.

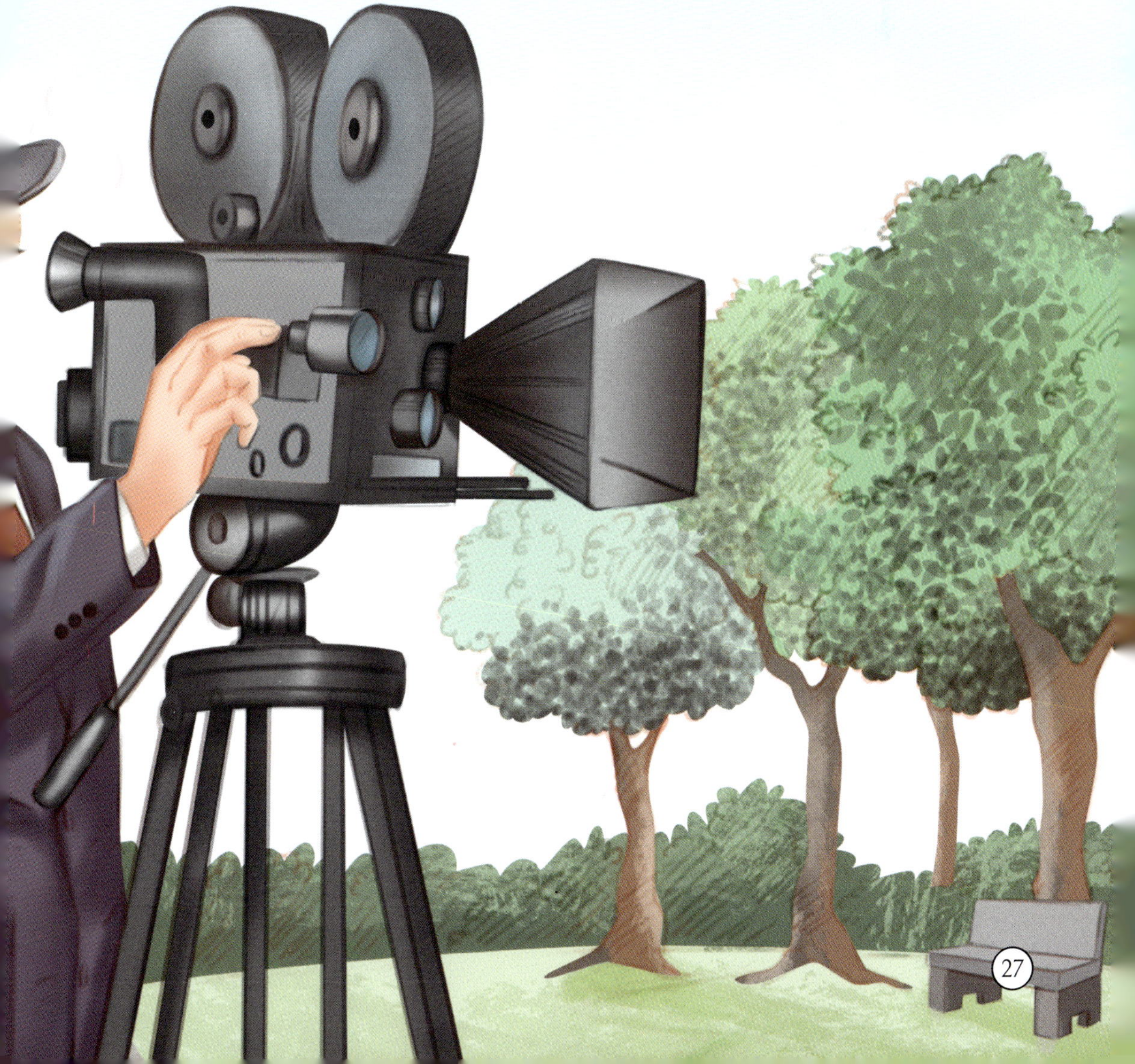

FINAL DAYS

Edison breathed his last on 18 October 1931. He died due to complications of diabetes. By this time, he had already left behind a league of inventions and a good deal of patents under his name. From 395 for electric light, 195 for the phonograph, 150 for the telegraph, 141 for storage batteries to 34 for telephone, he left a remarkable 1,093 patents under his name.

Not all of Edison's inventions were successful but he tried, despite the failures that came on his way, he kept trying with one motive: to make the life of humans comfortable and convenient with the help of science!

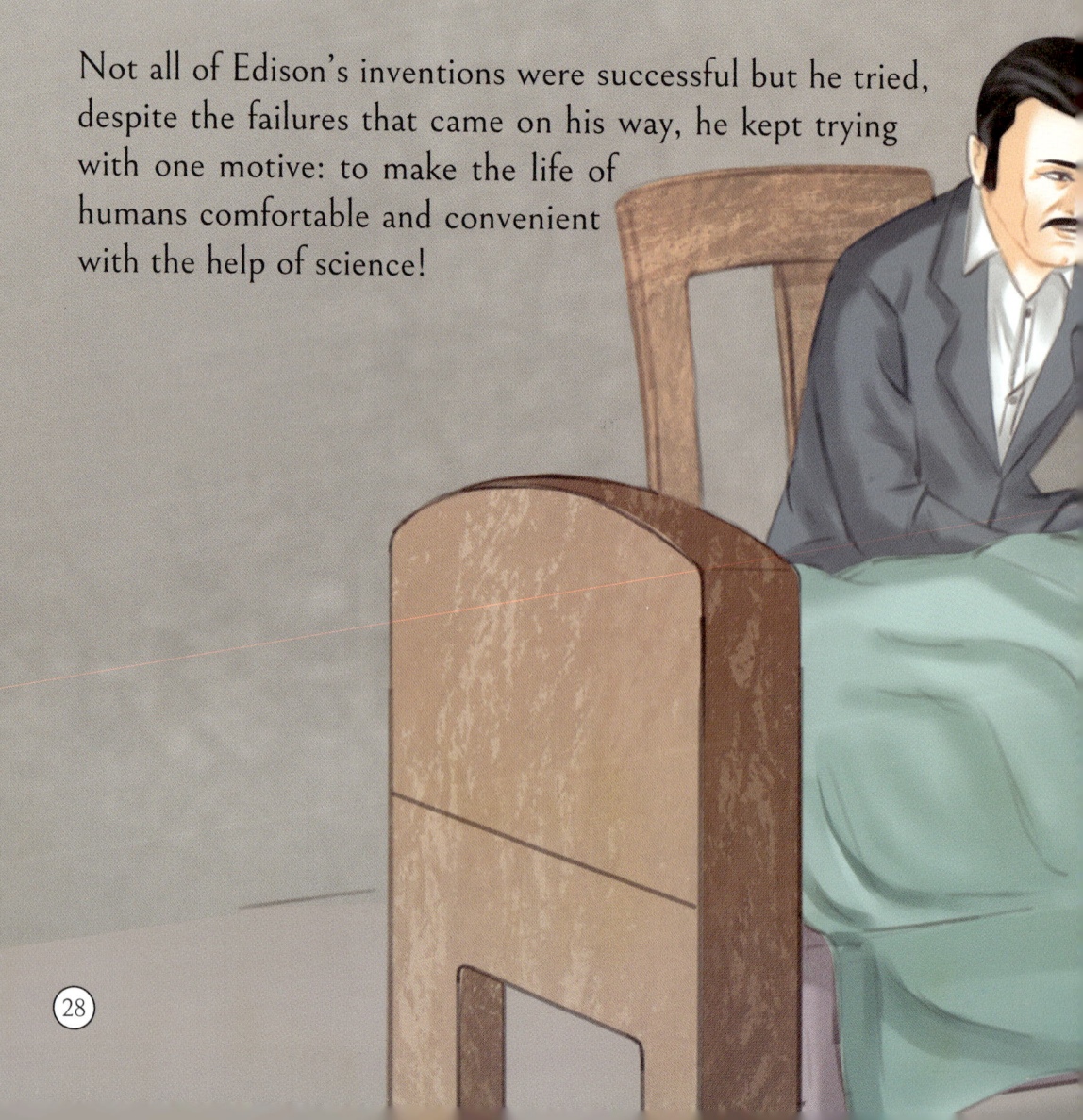

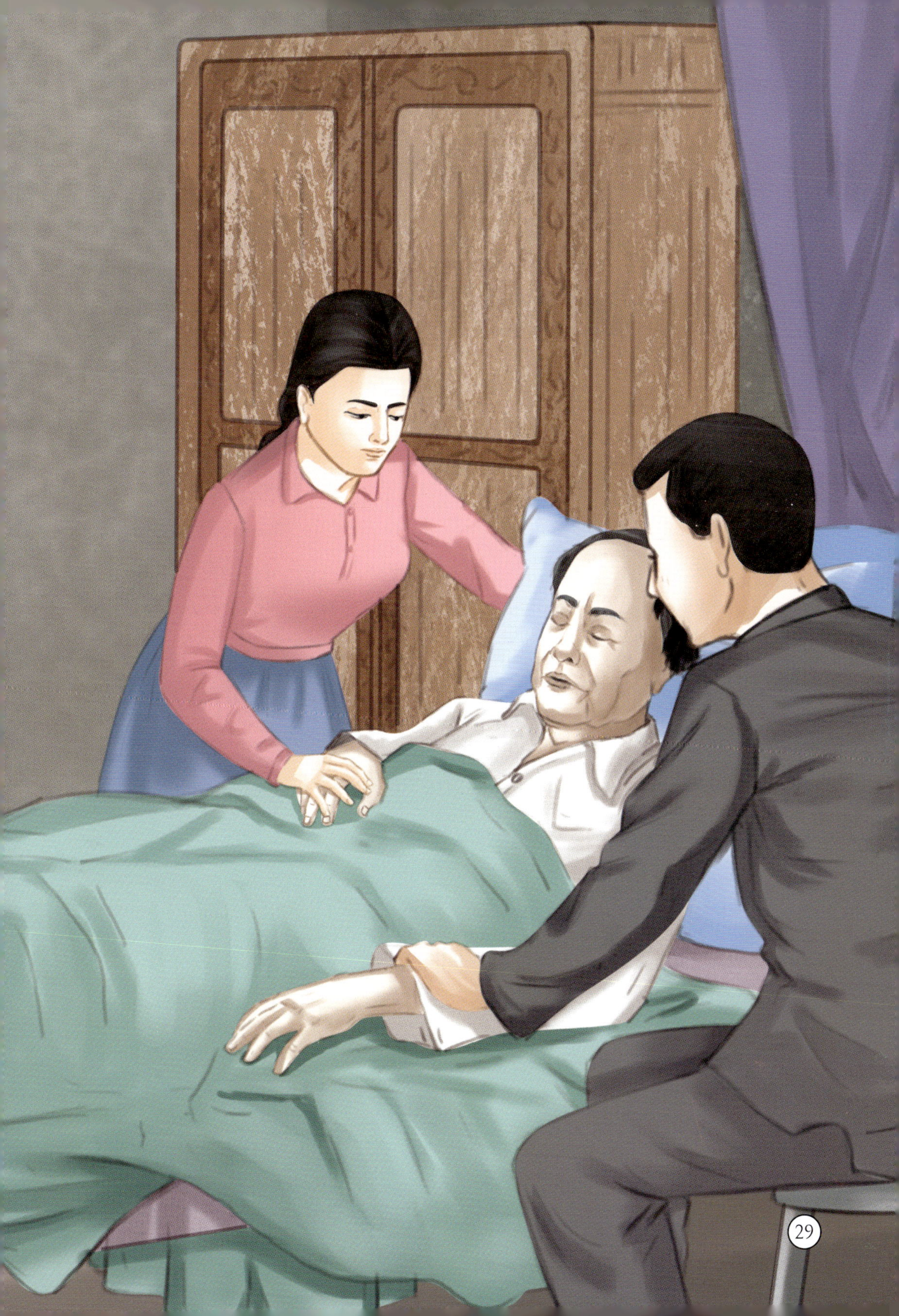

A NAME TO REMEMBER

Edison was quintessentially a born genius, who gifted the world with the most remarkable inventions, upon which he greatly improved. By the time he reached his mid-30s, he had already become one of the most famous men in America and was an inspiration to many; his story from rags to riches was a reflection of their big American dream which they aspired to achieve.

Edison's ingenuity finds shape in his work approach : his undeniable intelligence and passionate rigor gave him an edge over the formally trained scientists. It comes as no surprise that he was in constant conflict with the scientists and engineers who worked with him. Those who have worked with him, have described him a tyrant and some others have called him the most entertaining fellow to work with! Despite the diversity of opinions, one cannot deny that he was the man who formed the basis of applied research, and brought a technological and social revolution in the field of modern research.

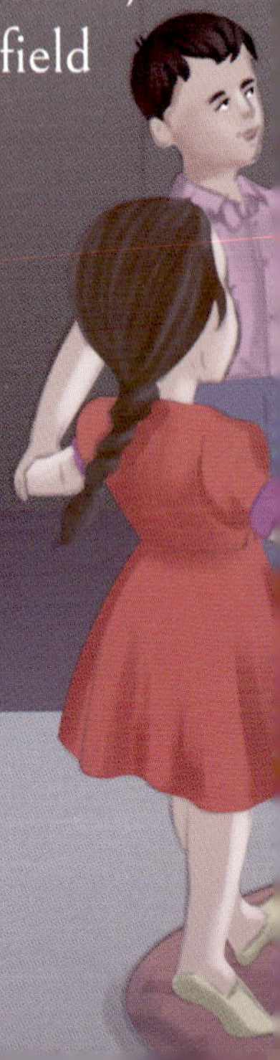

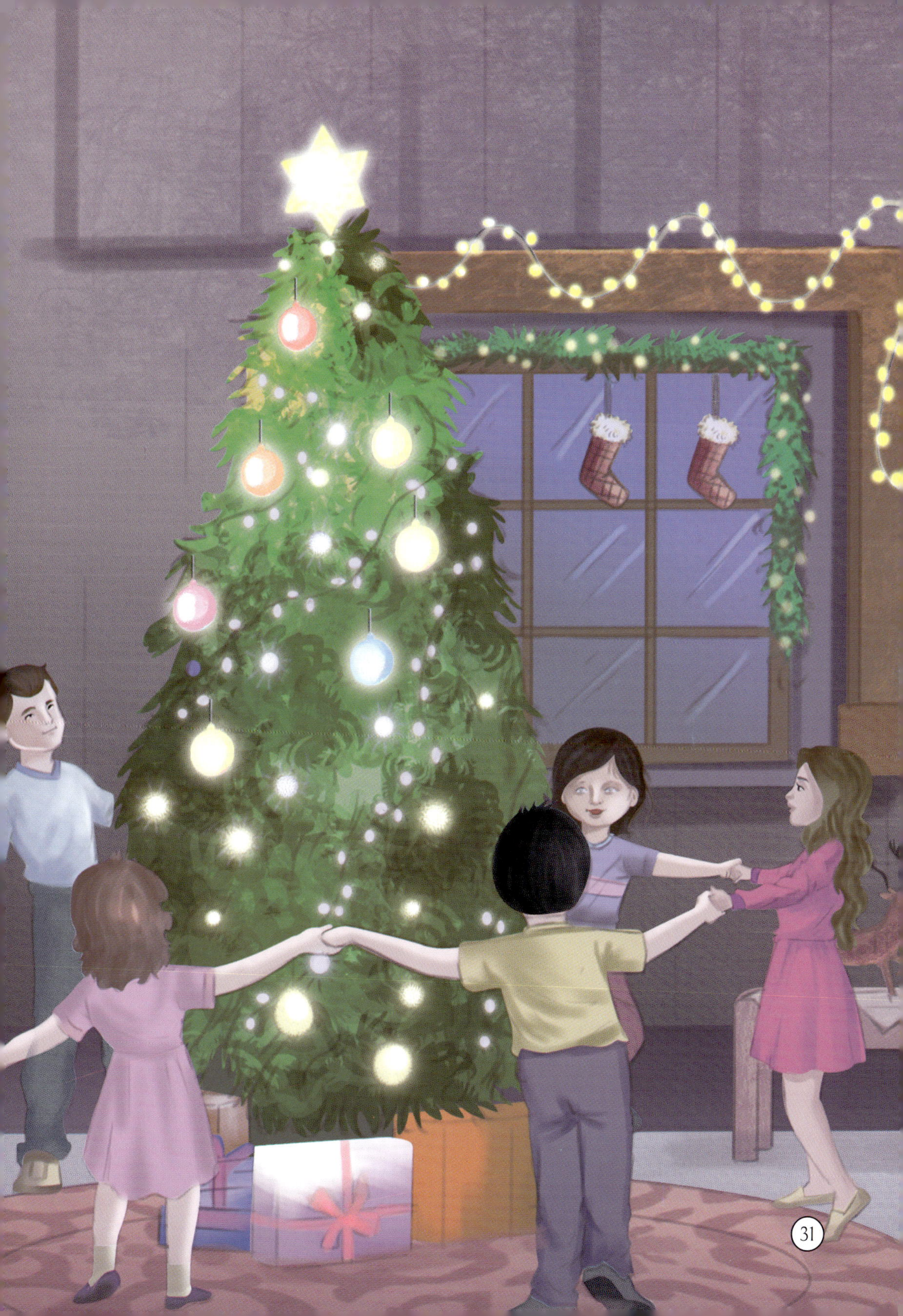

1847 : Thomas Edison is Born in Milan, Ohio

1863 : Edison sells newspapers and sundries on train between Port Huron, Michigan, and Detroit

1866 : Starts working as a telegraph operator at Western Union

1869 : Edison patents his first invention, an electric vote recorder

1871 : Edison marries Mary Stilwell

1877 : Invention of phonograph

1879 : Improvement of incandescent lamp

1880 : Establishes Edison Illuminating Company

1884 : Death of first wife Mary Stilwell

1886 : Marries Mina Miller

1887 : Establishes newer, larger laboratory at West Orange, New Jersey;
Beginning of War of Current era

1888 : Invention of motion pictures

1931 : Thomas Edison dies in West Orange, New Jersey